Cirencester College Library
Fosse Way Campus
Stroud Road
Cirencester
GL7 1XA

Project Risk
Assessment
in a week

DONALD TEALE

D1439932

Cirencester College, GL7 1XA
Telephone: 01285 640994

...oughton

...EADLINE GROUP

333778

As the champion of management, the
Chartered Management Institute shapes and
supports the managers of tomorrow. By sharing
intelligent insights and setting standards in
management development, the Institute helps
to deliver results in a dynamic world.

chartered

management

institute

inspiring leaders

For more information call 01536 204222 or visit www.managers.org.uk

Orders: please contact Bookpoint Ltd, 130 Milton Park, Abingdon, Oxon OX14 4SB.
Telephone: (44) 01235 827720, Fax: (44) 01235 400454. Lines are open from 9.00–6.00,
Monday to Saturday, with a 24 hour message answering service.
Email address: orders@bookpoint.co.uk

British Library Cataloguing in Publication Data
A catalogue record for this title is available from The British Library

ISBN 0 340 84972 X

First published	2001
Impression number	10 9 8 7 6 5 4 3 2 1
Year	2007 2006 2005 2004 2003

Copyright © 2001, 2003 Donald Teale

Cover image: Image Bank/Getty Images

All rights reserved. No part of this publication may be reproduced or transmitted in any
form or by any means, electronic or mechanical, including photocopy, recording, or any
information storage and retrieval system, without permission in writing from the publisher
or under licence from the Copyright Licensing Agency Limited. Further details of such
licences (for reprographic reproduction) may be obtained from the Copyright Licensing
Agency Limited, of 90 Tottenham Court Road, London W1P 9HE.

Typeset by SX Composing DTP, Rayleigh, Essex.
Printed in Great Britain for Hodder & Stoughton Educational, a division of Hodder
Headline Plc, 338 Euston Road, London NW1 3BH.

CONTENTS

Projects undertaken in today's competitive environment are subject to tight constraints and great uncertainties – the key ingredients of risk.

Project managers have a responsibility to deliver their project on time and under budget. Very few project managers achieve this, mainly due to the occurrence of unanticipated risks.

Following a few simple steps, project managers can forearm themselves by identifying and planning for the unexpected, thus greatly enhancing their chances of success. These steps are:

- Initiation
- Identification
- Assessment
- Analysis
- Reporting
- Producing a Risk Management Plan

What is project risk assessment?

Initiation

Today we will examine the first step for undertaking a risk assessment – initiation. The chapter's objective is to help you:

- understand the principles of a risk assessment
- understand the benefits
- identify the deliverables
- test the project's suitability

What is a risk assessment?

In this book, we will look at how to undertake a risk assessment as opposed to risk management, an ongoing process. A commonly accepted definition of a project risk is given by the APM in the *Project Risk Assessment and Management Guide*:

An uncertain event or set of circumstances, which should it occur, will have an effect on the achievement of the project's objectives.

It is fairly likely that during the course of a project some of these uncertain events will occur. The object of the risk assessment is to identify, quantify and, in some way, mitigate these events.

The risk assessment is a 'snapshot' of the project at a particular moment in time and can be divided into two stages:

1 Identifying and recording the risks along with their associated impacts. This stage can be considered as *the words* and is known as the qualitative stage.
2 Modelling the effect of the uncertainty on the project's schedule, cost and performance. This stage can be considered as *the numbers* and is known as the quantitative stage.

The term 'Risk Management' is used in this book for the ongoing process of reviewing and mitigating the identified risks in line with the recommendations of the risk assessment report.

The qualitative stage

We cover the activities for this stage on Monday and Tuesday. It involves a brainstorming session with the senior members of the project as well as the main stakeholders to identify potential risks to the project and to assign the risks to an individual or group within the project.

The list of identified risks is then entered into a 'risk register'. For each risk, we will record the likelihood of occurrence and impact on time, cost and performance using a scale from low to high.

A combination of the likelihood and impact is used to characterise each risk with a score. This pseudo-quantitative technique allows the risks to be ranked in order so that we can develop risk management action plans for each of the highest priority risks.

These plans should aim to do one of the following:

- Eliminate the risk entirely
- Reduce the impact of the risk
- Transfer the risk to another party better able to control it
- Accept and manage the risk.

The risk register will normally be stored in a computer database and can be used as a learning tool and checklist for future projects of a similar nature.

The quantitative stage
The second, quantitative, stage incorporates variability by translating the risk issues into a risk model. The risk model is developed to help you to understand the combined impact of project risks on the project's objectives. The risk model is normally based on actual information about the projects, such as an existing cost estimate and schedule.

We can then analyse the risk model using a Monte Carlo simulation tool, uncertainty being expressed in terms of a probability distribution that reflects a particular risk or risks.

The model is then simulated thousands of times, randomly sampling from the input distributions to give a range of possible outcomes. This is covered in much more detail on Wednesday, when we create our model. **And remember – it is not as complicated as it sounds!**

The benefits

The main benefit of undertaking a risk assessment is to give the project manager confidence that all eventualities which could affect the project have been considered.

The Monte Carlo simulation technique will produce a range of expected costs and durations which can be used to help us develop more realistic project targets.

Project targets are often imposed by external parties or requirements, such as time to market or a customer's needs. In such circumstances, a risk assessment will give you a true indication of your chances of success.

In alliance-type contracts, the risk assessment can be used to set the target price at a fair level and distribute the management of the risks to the most appropriate party.

Finally, the results of the assessment can be used to specify the appropriate levels of contingency that should be allocated to the budget.

A summary of the key benefits of undertaking a risk assessment

- Helps the Project team focus on the key issues
- Identifies a range of total costs and completion dates
- Reducing the potential impact of various risks may increase the value of the investment

- Allows the project manager to develop more realistic project targets
- Helps identify contingency levels.

Deliverables

Confidence is our ultimate goal. We want to give the senior management, or the customer, confidence that while considering this investment opportunity, all the internal and external factors have been included in our analysis. This leads to a robust examination of the project, including all the events that could affect it throughout its life.

The physical deliverables include:

- A *Risk Register* – detailing the identified risks that could affect the project. The register forms the starting point of our risk management process to be implemented on the project, if sanctioned.
- *Quantitative results* – showing the range of possible costs, delivery dates and critical paths, and a range of possible returns. The results are normally displayed in graphical formats.
- A *Risk Assessment Report* – results are consolidated into a formal report, which details the implications of the results and highlights the top risks to the project as well as the key drivers of the project. The report should also list recommendations for reducing the overall risk to the project, with detailed actions for each of the major risks which should be managed in accordance with the company's risk management procedures.

The intention of the risk assessment is to achieve a good understanding of the risks involved and to ensure that they are managed to the benefit of the company.

Most importantly, the measures outlined above are demonstrated to deliver better value from the entire project management function.

Deliverable Check List

- Risk Register
- Assessment Results
- Risk Report

Timing

Risk should be considered right from the moment the project is first proposed, and managed with increasing sophistication as the project matures. A typical project life cycle is shown below.

Phase	Description of phase
Concept	A proposal has been submitted and is being tested to ensure that the business case is robust.
Feasibility	Having shown a benefit to the organisation, a small team will produce an initial estimate of the cost and schedule with assumptions on the scope and value of the benefits.
Project Definition	A project manager has been appointed and during this phase the

	requirements (scope) will be fully defined with a detailed cost and schedule estimate.
Implementation	The project manager will implement the project to deliver the business requirements as identified in the project definition.
Operations	Depending on the project, it may be passed to the operations arm of the organisation or closed down having fulfilled its objectives.

Risks should be considered right from the concept phase, even though this might only be in the form of a simple list. An example of this could be an assumption that at first appears to be quite innocuous but has massive consequences.

Let us take as an example of this a project to build a new football stadium. A Premier league side would probably need a capacity of around 50,000. However, the club could be demoted before the stadium is complete. The Madejski Stadium in Reading has had to deal with these types of issues.

Concept
During the early stages of the project we can use the risk process as a decision support tool – to decide whether or not to go ahead.

Feasibility
During the feasibility stage the risk analysis can consider both the negative and positive aspects of the project (commonly referred to as risks and opportunities). The results can be measured against the project's potential revenue in the form

of a business risk model, to ensure that the organisation receives an adequate return in order to justify the investment.

Project definition
During the project definition phase, the emphasis changes to focus on the actual plan. This involves developing mitigation or fallback plans with trigger points to ensure that, before the bulk of the money starts to be spent, everything has been done to ensure a smooth passage for the project manager. During the definition phase, it is likely that the quality of data (particularly the cost estimate and schedule) will be substantially improved and this will allow us to make similar improvements to the risk model.

Implementation
This is the phase in the project where the 'real' work is tackled, eg building work. Risk assessments are undertaken here to ensure that the project is keeping close to the plan and that the completion date and budget are still realistic.

Operational
Operational risk management is beyond the scope of this book, but it suffices to say that this would be more related to such things as disaster recovery plans, feed stock and just-in-time management.

The risk process should grow with the project.

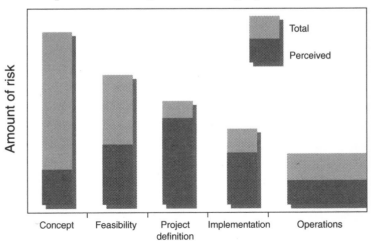

The chart above shows a typical path through a project. During the conceptual stage we have a limited view of the project and can only see the most obvious risks. When we move into the feasibility stage, many of the obvious risks are mitigated through planning and re-design. However, through closer examination of the project we have now identified more of the risks, thus increasing our perception of risk. The business should also develop Business Continuity Plans, ie processes for maintaining business as normal should a major risk occur.

During the project definition phase we should have a detailed plan with the majority of the risks visible. As we move through implementation, many of the early risks become obsolete, and a few more practical risks associated with the doing activities will exist. During operations there will always be the risks that we have identified and have recovery plans for; and those that we have not, such as a fuel crisis.

A summary of the levels suggested for each phase is shown in the table on the following page:

Phase	Level of risk assessment
Concept	A list of risks that should be taken into consideration with the project
Feasibility	A full risk assessment concentrating on the extreme results in order to be aware of the maximum exposure of the organisation
Project definition	A detailed qualitative and quantitative risk assessment focusing on target setting, contingency allocations and the cost/benefits of mitigation actions
Implementation	Full qualitative and quantitative risk assessments concentrating on the emergent items and changes from the previous assessment
Operations	Disaster recovery plans Business Continuity plans

Getting started

Tomorrow, you will kick off the risk identification phase with a brainstorming session. Your first task will be to prepare a short presentation to explain to your colleagues why you plan to take up a lot of their time undertaking this exercise.

Data Gathering

Objectives

Today we will hold the brainstorming session. This is intended, primarily, to get a rough list of the risks to the project, and it is an opportunity to get the members of the team to start thinking about risk.

Useful preparation

The first thing that you should prepare for today's session is a short presentation to explain the mission on which you are about to embark. The presentation should last for about ten minutes. The presentation should include reasons for undertaking the assessment, the objectives of the exercise and the assessment process, as well as explaining how the brainstorming session will work and why it will be necessary to hold follow up interviews.

Quick introductory presentation
- What is risk assessment?
- The process
  - Initiation
  - Identification
  - Assessment
  - Analysis
  - Reporting
- The objectives of the brainstorming
- Follow-up interviews

One of the main reasons for running a brainstorming session is to allow the group to build on ideas generated by others. The success of the brainstorming will, in part, rely on attendees, as well as your ability to guide them towards the desired outcome.

Who should attend?
Groups should consist of at least the key members of the project team: the head of each discipline. A variety of personnel can benefit the session and, often, a fresh set of eyes will spot loose ends. There should be between six and fifteen attendees. If more attend, the group tends to lose focus and many of the attendees lose interest. If any fewer than six attend you may get a very narrow view of the project.

Representatives from the customer, suppliers or sub-contractors generally enhance the session, giving the group an alternative perspective. You must watch out for the following types of disruptive individuals, though.

- *The dominator* – a very opinionated person who will not allow others in the group to express their views.
- *The nitpicker* – a person within the group who will attempt to hold up the whole process on the minutiae of detail. For example, arguing for hours over the definition of a 'High' risk.
- *The solver* – someone who forgets that the object of the brainstorming exercise is to identify risks not solutions.
- *The unbeliever* – an individual who was particularly close to the conception of the project and feels that all the risks identified are criticsms of the original project team. This individual will not accept that any risk still exists on the project, usually coming out with the stock answer of

'That's not a risk, we've covered that.' Although this may be true, it quickly intimidates the other members of the group and stifles the flow of ideas.

The rules of brainstorming
There are only a couple of rules in brainstorming, the first is:

All individuals are equal.

A session that is dominated by the project manager is unlikely to be productive. It is up to you to ensure that this rule is enforced and that the company hierarchy is left at the door.

No idea is too stupid to be mentioned.

All the risks identified should be noted and no criticism should be allowed of any idea. The point is to generate many ideas, not refine a few. In many cases where a risk is not valid, and is eventually excluded from the analysis, it may lead to additional undiscovered risks.

The purpose of the session is to identify risks *not* solutions.

Much time can be wasted on trying to identify solutions that can be addressed using a smaller group at a later stage.

Getting started
This can be very difficult, and it is always good to have a couple of risks up your sleeve to get the ball rolling. Before the brainstorming session you should have read any documentation relating to the project, such as the proposal or any progress reports that have been produced, noting any points you think may lead to risk.

Timing
Ideally, the session should last between one and two hours. If it looks like lasting substantially longer then you should consider splitting up the group and/or running several smaller sessions.

Note-taking
One of the most successful methods of note-taking is to use a flip chart and copious amounts of Blue Tack or drawing pins. A nominated member of the group stands by the flip chart recording each risk as it is fired out from the group. On average you can expect anywhere between 20 and 60 risks to be identified during the session.

Other problems to watch out for are:

- 'Limited horizons,' where the group concentrates only on the current phase, and
- 'Tunnel vision,' where they only consider their own aspects of the project, ignoring any external parties not represented at the brainstorming.

One way to mitigate against the last two pitfalls is to use a matrix of the stakeholders and project phases or areas, as shown below:

Stakeholders

	Client	Project team	Suppliers	Manufacturers	External
Concept					
Feasibility					
Project definition					
Implementation					
Operations					

Towards the end of the session, quickly run through each of the boxes to ensure that all aspects have been considered.

Checklists can help structure the process by dividing issues into categories such as contractual or political issues. The checklist should include areas that traditionally cause problems in your industry. These can be developed by experienced project managers using hindsight or by collecting risks from previous projects.

Closing the session
The end of the session will be heralded by the drying up of new ideas. It is always worthwhile cutting the session off before they completely run out of steam, and quickly asking

each person in turn, around the table, whether there was anything they thought of that hadn't been mentioned. This is useful to ensure that the quieter members of the group have an opportunity to air their views.

Remember to remind all the attendees that new risks can be added to the register later. If you have time, it is useful to quickly assign the identified risks to individuals within the group – this will help with the follow up interviews.

Risk criteria

Quite often the start of a brainstorming session is an ideal opportunity to define the risk criteria. From reading the project documents you should have an idea of what the levels should be. However, it helps the group focus on the main issues if you set out at the start of the meeting exactly what you mean by a high, medium or low risk impact, and the likelihood of occurrence.

This can also be noted on the flip chart and pinned on the wall. The impacts can be defined as either percentages or absolute values, and there should be references to both cost and time.

	Impacts	Likelihood
High	20–100%	70–100%
Medium	10–20%	30–70%
Low	0–10%	0–30%

Summary

You should now be in receipt of several sheets of a flip chart, probably in illegible hand writing, listing your first set of risks.

Everyone in the team is now eagerly awaiting your results.

Producing the risk register

Today we will be looking at how to:

> • Store the risks in a register that can be distributed to the relevant project members and included in the risk report
> • Be able to group the risks by meaningful categories
> • Be able to rank the risks by severity.

The first priority of the analyst is to get the risks into some sort of manageable order, which will allow us to draw some general conclusions from the qualitative risk analysis. Although it is possible to generate a paper-based system such as a card file, a computer is the only real practical option.

Risk fields

The information on each risk can be stored in fields. A field is a descriptor of a type of information. For example, take a name 'Richard Bailey'; this data can be divided into a First Name (Richard) and a Surname (Bailey). The fields associated with the name are 'First Name' and 'Surname'.

The number of fields that you can associate with a risk item is almost boundless, but you must remember to be practical. A form that is overly onerous will lose the attention of the reader, and greatly increase the time taken to maintain the register.

Bearing in mind the need for brevity, a few suggested fields are listed below in order of importance. It is very unlikely that you will require the full set.

Descriptors
The following fields are the main descriptors, and on small projects could be sufficient detail for the entire database.

- **Title**
  This should be a one line, brief description of the risk. The title should give a clear indication of what the risk actually is, not a cryptic clue.

- **Description**
  This is your opportunity to detail exactly the issues involved in this risk. The description should also contain the process that is being undertaken in mitigation of the risk.

- **Likelihood**
  This is the chance that this risk will occur. Risks are, by definition, uncertain events. As touched upon on Monday, the easiest way to apply this field is to use banding, such as 'High', 'Medium' and 'Low'.

- **Impact**

  The impact, like the likelihood, can be grouped into 'High', 'Medium' and 'Low' bands. In its simplest form, the impact will be a combination of severity in terms of cost, time and performance. A more sophisticated method is to separate out the impacts on the various components of the project, such as the Cost, Time and Quality.

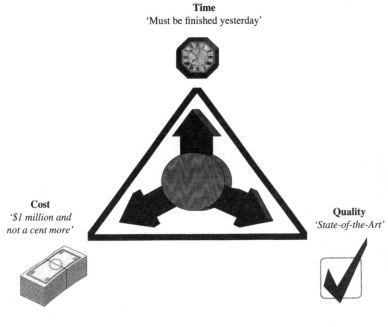

Time
'Must be finished yesterday'

Cost
*'$1 million and
not a cent more'*

Quality
'State-of-the-Art'

- **Cost**

  The cost can be divided into actual values or percentage values representing change on budgets, eg a high risk could be a 50% increase on the budget or a £5 million one-off cost.

- **Time**

  This is generally delay to the schedule; ie how late will my project be if this risk occurs? It is hard to quantify exactly how long the project will be delayed by a particular risk occurring. However, as you will find out, much of the qualitative work is based on educated guessing. The secret is to over- rather than under-estimate.

- **Quality**
  This is one of those soft issues which can be tailored to suit your project. It is used generally as a repository for all those risks that will have an impact on the project without affecting cost or schedule. Issues such as:

  'The product keeps breaking down due to cheap components.'

  Be careful here, as it is always better to describe the impacts in terms of cost or delay, as this is what grabs the project manager's attention. Many risks that you believe fit into the quality field could be translated into cost or schedule terms.

Risk categories
In addition to the main descriptor fields, we can also categorise the risks. This is done to highlight general trends that run through the risks, which can be used to identify strategic mitigation actions.

It is unlikely that a single risk could have supported the recruitment of a dedicated HR Manager. However, the risk assessment might show that the combined effect of all the HR risks could far exceed the salary of the HR manager.

- **Category**
  Although the title is a little bit generic, it is almost mandatory if you have more than twenty risks. It is a good idea to have a limited number of categories and the categories will probably

define themselves from the risks you have identified. One thing to always bear in mind when undertaking a risk assessment is that the object is to tell a story, and the categories should help support the narrative. The type of categories that you frequently see are: management, implementation, operations, technical, resources.

It is fairly common to have arguments over assigning particular risks to individual categories, but if you define the rules early and base them on source, impact or management, you should be able to resolve the conflicts.

On particularly complex projects, you may want to delve further and have the risks divided into more detailed categories, such as:

- **Phase**
  The point in the project life cycle that the risk will hit. This would allow the manager to view the risks that are applicable to a particular phase. It would also allow risks that apply to phases that are complete to be easily closed.

  Phase is particularly useful during long projects when, although you want to concentrate on the most important risks, it gives you an indication of how long you have to implement mitigating actions.

You can also have deliverable items, milestones and sub-projects – the list could be endless.

Just remember though, all these fields have to be entered and maintained, so ask yourself if they really add value. Does this information add to the story, and will it help the project manager?

Management
This group of fields is relevant to the sponsor of the risk
assessment.

• **Nominee**
This field is pretty much compulsory, if you intend to use
the register as a tool to manage risks.

The definition of the nominee is: 'The person best able to
manage or monitor the risk.' This is the person you chase
for information relating to the risk.

Another two fields that can be added to the management
section are the Source and the Bearer. This again is another
level of sophistication, but extremely useful when your
project involves numerous third parties.

The Source is used to determine whose fault the risk is. For
example, the risk of 'Scope change' may be due to an
uncertain and unpredictable customer. The Bearer is the
party who suffers the consequence. Without a proper change
control procedure or agreed terms of reference, the Bearer of
the 'Scope change' risk will be the project. However, with a
good contract, this risk can be transferred back to the
customer.

If you use the same list of parties for the 'Source' and 'Bearer'
you can produce a matrix showing the distribution of risks.

This will help identify guilty parties in the distribution of risk
throughout the project. Your recommendations will no doubt
suggest a more equal distribution and an example of this will
be covered in the reports section on Friday.

	Client	Project team	Suppliers	Manufacturers	External
Client	5	10		1	
Project team	1	34	4		
Suppliers	5	12			
Manufacturers	2	10			
External		5			

Bearer (column header group)

Source (row header group)

Each box displays the number of risks

Responses

Identifying the risks is only half the story; having to suffer the impact of an unforeseen event may be considered unlucky, but to suffer from the impact of an event that you saw coming is negligent. You will need therefore a field that includes your response to the risk.

You can take one or a combination of four generic actions:

- *Transfer* – pass the risk on to someone who is better able to manage it;
- *Eliminate* – develop a plan or series of actions that will prevent the risk from occurring;
- *Mitigate* – develop a plan or series of actions that will reduce the probability of the risk occurring and/or the impact if the risk does happen;
- *Accept* – in some cases, it will not be possible to mitigate the risk and you should prepare a contingency or a fallback plan should the risk occur.

You can have one field for each of the four actions; or you can lump the responses into two groups:

- *Mitigation actions* – which deals with proactive steps to reduce the likelihood or impact of the risk; and/or
- *Fallback plans* – which accept the likelihood of the risk occurring and put in place a set of plans that will be implemented should the worst happen. This is sometimes known as contingency planning.

A common problem with mitigation actions is that they can be too vague and just describe the risk owner or nominee carrying on as normal. Actions such as 'Good communication' or 'Better liaison with third party providers', are unlikely to be carried out. Again, we can introduce more levels of sophistication by turning the rather vague good intentions into definitive actions with an actionee and a deadline. The project manager or nominee can then report on the progress of these actions.

Scoring systems

One of the main purposes of having a risk register is to rank the risks. This will allow you to produce a list of the top ten risks, which gives the project manager the opportunity to focus on the really important risks.

Scoring systems come in many forms, and it is likely that this will prove an area of keen debate. The system outlined in this book is not the only one possible. However, it does work and has been used on projects with budgets of several million to a couple of billion. Other techniques will be touched on, but remember the common theme: **Don't make it too complicated to manage**.

The recommended method – The P-I Matrix

The recommended method in this book is to use a Probability – Impact Matrix. We have already scored the likelihood of the risk occurring as a High, Medium or Low chance, based on ranges of probabilities such as greater than 70%, between 30% and 70% and less than 30%. We have also scored the impacts in a similar manner, High, Medium or Low, relating to either actual values or percent increases on the costs, schedule or quality.

The P-I Matrix involves producing a grid that contains each combination of probability and impact. Each option is then assigned a value, as shown below. If you have an impact score for each of the impact types, eg Cost, Schedule and Quality, I recommend that you take the worst score from the cost, schedule and quality criteria for your ranking.

Probability–Impact Matrix

Probability		Low	Medium	High
	High	4	7	9
	Medium	2	6	8
	Low	1	3	5
		Low	Medium	High

Impact

It is inadvisable to sum the scores of the impact categories (ie cost, schedule and quality), as our scores do not take into consideration severity of impact. For example, let us consider a one million pound construction project, on which there are only two risks.

The first risk involves a high chance that the crane we hired for a major lift is not able to perform the lift but hiring a bigger crane would cost the project two hundred thousand pounds more. This is obviously a high cost risk, which could increase the budget by twenty percent. However, this risk will not affect the schedule or the quality/performance of the project since a larger crane is available, and the load will be lifted.

The second risk relates to the delivery of equipment that has to be lifted by the crane. There is a medium likelihood risk that due to inclement weather the delivery of the equipment will be delayed. The weather data for previous years has been studied and the lift has been scheduled for September, which is normally a good month. However, there is a small chance that winter will come early and there will be difficulties in getting the equipment to the site. The cost impact will be high with the need to extend the hire of the crane. The schedule delay will also be high, especially if the project has to wait until the following summer.

Compare the two risks in the table below:

Risk 1 – Crane is too small		
Impact Area	Prob – Imp	Score
Quality	Nil – Nil	0
Schedule	Nil – Nil	0
Cost	High – High	9
	Sum	9

From the tables, risk 2 appears the most severe. However, many project managers would consider risk 1 to be the worst as it has a much higher cost impact.

Risk 2 – Difficulties in getting the equipment to the site		
Impact Area	Prob – Imp	Score
Quality	Nil – Nil	0
Schedule	High – Medium	7
Cost	High – Low	4
	Sum	11

Other scoring methods

Even simpler P–I Matrix
There is another method that is used fairly frequently, which is simpler than the P–I Matrix recommended above. This is the simple multiplication of the probability and impact. The Low, Medium and High scores for both probability and impact are scored one, two and three respectively, and the two numbers are multiplied together. This also gives a range from 1 to 9 as shown in the table below:

Probability–Impact Matrix

Probability			Impact		
High	3	3	6	9
Medium	2	2	4	6
Low	1	1	2	3
		Low 1	Medium 2	High 3

The disadvantages of this system become apparent when the number of risks grow. It is impossible to differentiate between certain large groups of risks, and leads to the debate as to whether a High Impact/Low Probability is more serious than a Low Impact/High Probability. Using this P–I system there will only be six groups of risks (9, 6, 4, 3, 2, 1).

A further disadvantage of this method is related to reporting. If the first P-I matrix is used, the reader can tell from the score where the risk sits on the matrix, hence reducing the amount of information you have to show on any report. It also helps to have unique numbers if you plan to write a macro to produce some of your charts, particularly if you want to map the risks directly onto the matrix.

Weighted P-I Matrix
One way that has been developed to overcome the problems of combining risk scores is to weight the different impact categories before summing them. So, on a project with a very politically sensitive completion date, such as an Olympic Stadium, you may decide that schedule risks are more serious than cost risks. The quality of the product may also be less important than achievement of the budget.

In this case the analyst can use either of the above methods and multiply the resultant number by the severity of the category.

Taking our crane example, if we are more concerned with cost than schedule we can weight the impact categories. For example, we could say that the schedule impact was half as important as the cost impact, and that the quality impact was half as important as the schedule impact. This would lead to factors of 4 x cost, 2 x schedule and 1 x quality. This would then alter our table.

Compare the two risks in the table below:

Risk 1 – Crane is too small

Impact Area	Prob – Imp	Score
Quality x 1	N – N	0
Schedule x 2	N – N	0
Cost x 4	H – H	36
	Sum	36

Risk 2 – Difficulties in getting the equipment to the site

Impact Area	Prob – Imp	Score
Quality x 1	N – N	0
Schedule x 2	H – M	14
Cost x 4	H – L	16
	Sum	30

The first risk, with its higher cost impact, now becomes more important. This can be considered a dangerous game to play. There is no substitute for taking each risk on its own merits and applying common sense. However, more complex methods are more difficult to display graphically.

Tools – the technical bit

There are three main options for storing the data and each option has its pros and cons. The list below starts with what I believe to be the simplest and then graduates to the most complex method.

Spreadsheets

The simplest way to store the data is in a spreadsheet. The amount of functionality you can get from your spreadsheet risk register will depend on your knowledge and the dexterity of your chosen package. The fields can be placed along the top row and the data entered in the rows below.

The main advantage of this method is speed. If you don't have many risks and only summary descriptions, a spreadsheet may be all that is necessary.

On the downside, a spreadsheet is really a numerical tool and the risk register is primarily text based. So eventually, you will find that some of the boxes just aren't big enough for all the text you want to enter, or you may find it difficult to produce reports in an acceptable format.

Word processors

There are two ways you can use your word processor to produce a risk register, and which one you select will depend on your level of competence and the quality of output that you require.

You can simply create a proforma and fill in the details of each risk on a separate form.

However, a much better way to do it is to make use of the mail merge options and create primary and secondary files. The secondary file contains the raw data in a uniform format, normally a table, and the primary file contains the layout of the report that you require. By using the mail merge, you will not become constrained by the method of entry, and you will be able to produce full or summary reports and reports for particular individuals or groups. Please refer to your word processor manual for a better explanation of mail merging.

Databases

There are numerous levels of relational databases, from the simple PC based Microsoft Access to the much larger Oracle based systems.

Only create a database if it is a very long project or if you are likely to undergo this process fairly often. A lot of money is wasted by large organisations developing complex databases which become projects in their own right. However, most projects are slightly different and it is hard to produce a 'one size fits all' database. In summary the reporting tools should be tailored to the project to avoid making too much work for the analyst.

Filling in the information

As you probably realise, we have generated a lot more fields than we can fill with the information we received from the brainstorming. So before you finish for the day, you will have

to print out your full risk register in Nominee order and visit each nominee with a copy of his or her risks to be completed.

You will probably have to chase the less co-operative members of your organisation for the detailed information.

Summary

Today we have produced the fundamental building block of your risk assessment. You should now be sitting back admiring a large pile of paper, containing your first-cut risk register, with the minimum number of fields you require.

Elsewhere in the project there are other members struggling to come up with mitigation plans for the risks they glibly identified on Monday.

Producing a risk model

Today's main objectives will be to:

- Understand a Monte Carlo simulation
- Produce a risk model that reflects the uncertainty in the project
- Understand the different ways in which you can model the risks that you have identified.

Monte Carlo simulation

The object of producing a risk model is to inject a degree of realism into plans. This is done by applying ranges of possible costs and durations to the deterministic (single point) estimates. The ranges are called input distributions and are covered in more detail later today. For now, we will only consider the simplest input distribution: the triangular distribution.

Triangular distributions consist of three values: a minimum, most likely and a maximum value. The probability of any particular value occurring increases at a linear rate from the minimum to the most likely value and then decreases at a (possibly) different linear rate from most likely to maximum. If you draw this distribution out you get a triangle shape, hence its name.

The best way to understand a Monte Carlo simulation is by example. Let's consider a very simple project: 'The Shed Project'.

Objectives
- To procure and assemble a garden shed during the next bank holiday week end

Materials
- A flat-packed shed from a local DIY shop
- A number of patio slabs on which to site the shed
- Sand and cement to lay the slabs

Other costs
- Transportation of the materials from shop to home

Assumptions
- All the fixings for the shed will be included in the kit

We can start by putting together a rough estimate of the costs:

Item	Cost
Shed (6 x 3 feet)	£100
Slabs (21)	£42
Sand	£6
Cement	£6
Van hire	£15
Total	**£169**

This estimate is fairly poor because it was undertaken without reference to any primary data such as shop catalogues or adverts. However, I need to have a rough estimate quickly because I want to withdraw the cash before the weekend. So how much money do I take out?

Many industries use a rule of thumb, such as:

Project estimate based on actual price +/-10%

Project estimate with no supporting data +/-20%

However, using a Monte Carlo simulation, we hope to get a better grasp of what the likely cost could be, and what we could expect to pay.

In the example we are only going to include the risk of estimating uncertainty, ie we will exclude specific risks, such as:

- Your partner decides the shed needs to be painted in sympathy with the garden, hence adding a can of paint to your estimate.
- The shop has sold out of 6x3 sheds and you have to buy one 10x4 which is more expensive.

So our next step is to consider each of the line items in our estimate and apply a range of possible costs. As we are only considering triangular distributions, this will be in the form of a minimum, most likely and maximum cost.

You must bear in mind that the minimum and maximum values should be the extremes. For example, in our first line entry, it might be possible that some stores in the town are offering sheds at a discount, particularly since it is a bank holiday weekend. Ever the optimist, I have estimated a possible fifty percent discount, so my minimum cost is £50, but I could be unlucky and shed prices may have risen and the shed might cost me £125. However, I am pretty confident in my original estimate, so my most likely value will remain at £100.

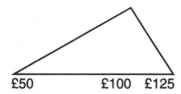

£50   £100   £125

You can tell from the shape of the triangle that I am obviously expecting some form of discount. (The centre of gravity of the triangle will be less than £100, £91.67 to be precise.)

Carrying on down my list of materials, I can enter distributions for all the items.

Item	Cost	Minimum	Most likely	Maximum
Shed (6 x 3 feet)	£100	£50	£100	£125
Slabs (21)	£42	£30	£42	£63
Sand	£6	£5	£6	£8
Cement	£6	£5	£6	£8
Van hire	£15	£10	£15	£20
Total	**£169**			

So now we have a very simple risk model which only considers the risk of estimating uncertainty.

The simulation tool will run through the project thousands of times, randomly selecting values between the minimum and maximum rather like a roulette wheel – hence the name Monte Carlo. Because of the shape of the distribution, values close to the most likely value are more likely to be selected than those near the minimum or maximum. After many iterations, the distribution of values selected should approach the defined triangle shape.

I have tried to show this diagrammatically in the table below. Each run of the simulation is called an iteration. On the first iteration the computer has selected £60 for the price of the shed, £30 for the slabs, £5 for the sand and so on. On the second run the shed costs £100 and so on.

Note that the computer doesn't just choose values in whole numbers of pounds, but we have rounded the values to the nearest pound to make it simpler to read. The usual number of iterations is about 3,000, so that would be difficult to undertake with a set of dice and a piece of paper.

Item	Run					
	1	2	3	4	5	—
Shed (6 x 3 feet)	60	100	105	55	80	—
Slabs (21)	30	38	45	58	40	—
Sand	5	6	6	7	8	—
Cement	6	6	5	8	7	—
Van hire	12	11	15	14	20	—
Total	**113**	**161**	**176**	**142**	**155**	—

We can see from this simple example that there is quite a range of possible costs. By running thousands of iterations, the computer will build of a picture of all, or at least most, of the possible outcomes and the percentage likelihood of each outcome being achieved.

We could plot a graph of the results of the simulation for any particular line item, for example the shed costs. The different possible costs are shown along the x-axis, and the bars in the chart below show the number of times each cost was selected. So by the end of the simulation, the shed cost of £70 (which actually equates to a value between £67.50 and £72.50) is selected just over 150 times (from the y-axis).

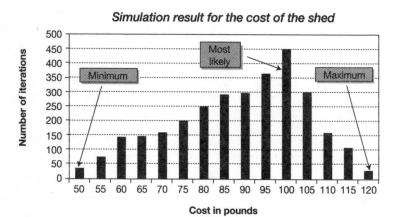

Simulation result for the cost of the shed

We can see that the model has followed our instructions and the results resemble a triangle with a minimum price of £50, a maximum price of £120 and a most likely price of £100. The most likely price is the price corresponding to the most number of iterations, ie the highest bar. The expected cost, which is the arithmetical mean of the results, would be about £90; (£50 x 34 iterations + £55 x 70 its + £60 x 135 + ...) divided by 3000.

When you combine all the line items (the shed, slabs and cement, etc) you get a much smoother chart like the one shown below:

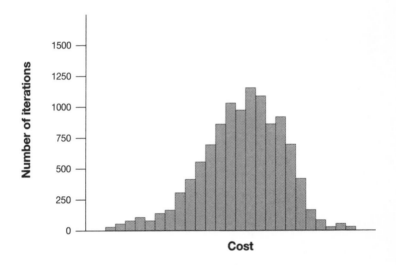

The real benefit of this chart is unleashed when you plot the cumulative distributions as a percentage. That means adding all the results sequentially until the last bar is the sum of all the others.

This will be the total number of simulations, ie three thousand in this case. Since this still does not tell us anything of particular interest, we take each point as a percentage of the total. If the last point shown on the graph above represents 625 iterations, the value we plot is $625/3000 \times 100 = 20.83\%$.

Once all the points are calculated (and luckily a computer can work out the values for you) we can then draw a line through all the points and get one of the most useful results of a risk analysis yet, commonly known as an 'S-Curve', as shown below:

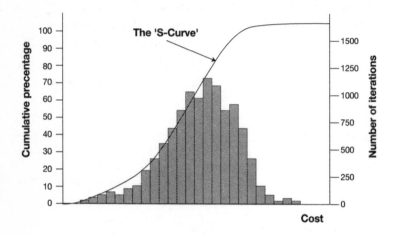

The S-Curve now shows you the probability of each cost being achieved, however, you will have to wait until tomorrow to find out exactly how useful this curve is. For now, we have to get on with the business of producing the risk model for your project.

Suitability of existing models (Cost/Schedule)

Usually the first thing to do when producing a risk model is to find out what the project already has. This will depend a lot on the level of maturity of the project. A project that is in its feasibility stage may not have too much information, whereas a project that is up and running should have budgets, schedules and progress reports.

The cost estimate should be broken down into a level of detail that matches the risks, and the schedule should be a series of logically linked activities.

It is always a good idea, to test the model in a deterministic mode, to check that the results match with the project team's expectations before you run the full analysis. If you have created your model by selecting the most likely values as equal to the estimate, then running a single iteration, and selecting the most likely value for each item in the risk model, should give you the same results as the estimate.

Mapping the risks

There are two distinct types of uncertainty that we can include in the risk model. These are known as: 'General uncertainty in the estimates'; and 'Specific risk impacts'.

General uncertainty in the estimates
In producing the cost or schedule estimate, the project manager has had to make many assumptions as to the state of the future. For example, if I noticed my car's fuel tank is nearly empty, I would try to find a garage to fill it up. I know roughly that it will cost about thirty pounds.

If I had to estimate the cost to within ten percent, I wouldn't have a chance. This is because:

- I don't know exactly how much fuel I will need to fill up the tank
- I don't know exactly how much the next garage will charge for the petrol
- Even the tax might have increased since the last time I visited a garage
- I don't how far away the next garage is, so I don't know how much more fuel I will use in getting there.

If there are so many factors at play in a fairly simple task such as estimating how much money I will need to fill up my car, it will be very much more difficult to estimate the cost of, say, building the Channel Tunnel or the Millennium Dome.

You will find yourself, when interviewing the persons responsible for putting together the estimates, that they will be very reluctant to admit to any variance on their estimates. Bearing this in mind, one way to help them consider the accuracy is to provide a list of points that would provide weight to their confidence, such as:

- Is the estimate based on firm prices received from suppliers?
- Is contingency built into your estimates?
- Do the estimates make allowances for inflation?
- Has the organisation undertaken similar tasks?

As with the car example, another question you must ask yourself is 'How important is this cost to the project?' As long as I intend to pay my fuel bill by credit card it doesn't really matter if I can only estimate the amount to an accuracy greater than ten percent. Applying this to a major project, the estimator should spend the highest proportion of his time pricing the key 'major' items of expenditure. The minor items can be roughly estimated and can have large amounts of uncertainty applied to them.

So how, exactly, do we apply this uncertainty?
Generally, cost uncertainty is applied in terms of a plus or minus percentage. For example, I thought that it would cost approximately £30 to fill up my car with petrol. Due to the factors mentioned previously, I could comfortably say that the estimate was within plus or minus 20 percent, ie the maximum cost I would expect to pay is £36 and the

minimum would be £24.

When it comes to producing the risk model, it is vitally important to be sure that you have captured the full range of possibilities.

Schedule risk uncertainty is applied in a similar way, if we take the same example of filling a car with petrol. A Formula One team can do it in about eight seconds; it will probably take me five minutes; however, there could be a queue and it could take up to fifteen minutes. So my range on the duration of filling up my car with petrol might be seven minutes minus two minutes plus eight minutes.

It is always a good idea to consider the ranges in actual times or costs, as well as percentages. It is easy for an interviewee to answer glibly plus or minus ten percent, but if we are talking about the price of a helicopter, at around five million, plus or minus ten percent hides the proportionate reality.

Specific risk impacts
These risks relate more closely to the register. In fact it is a good idea to relate the specific risk directly to the risk register, should anyone in the team start to ask difficult questions along the lines of 'Where did that cost come from?' One way of doing this is to include a 'How modelled' field in the register, which provides an audit trail from the register to the model.

Specific risks normally have two aspects: the likelihood of occurrence and the severity of the impact.

A common example of this is found in the oil and gas industry. When installing an oil rig at sea, many important items of equipment have to be lowered into position by a crane mounted on a barge. There are many documented cases of cranes dropping key items of equipment, which can cost up to five million dollars to repair or replace.

The oil rig example can be modelled as, say, a ten percent likelihood of occurrence with a possible impact of at best $100,000, most likely $500,000, and a worst cost of $1,000,000. The least expensive impact would be the crane dropping the item when it was only a short distance from the deck. The worst case would relate to a drop over the sea, where the item could be lost, with the associated costs of delay while awaiting a new part to be delivered.

So far we have only talked about three point estimates: a worst case, a most likely case and a best case. However, there are numerous other 'distributions' available to the professional statistician. In this book, we will only cover those that are likely to be most applicable to risk analysis exercises.

Uniform distributions
Uniform distributions are used when the cost or duration could be anywhere between two points, and you don't have a clue what the most likely value is. The simulation tool will, on each iteration, randomly select a value between the two extremes.

Discrete distributions
Discrete distributions are used when you have a set of discrete values that could be selected, like in an 'either or' situation. This can occur when you have a risk that may or may not occur. If it doesn't occur, there will be no cost impact; however, if it does occur it will cost you a flat fee of £100,000. Percentage likelihoods can be attached to each

value, for example there might be an 80% chance of the risk costing zero and a 20% chance that the risk will cost £100,000. The percentages when summed should be equal to 100.

Custom distributions
Custom distributions can be used when you have specific data on which to base your model and/or the data cannot be easily be fitted to one of the standard statistical distributions.

A good example of the use of a custom distribution can be found in the oil and gas industry. A pipeline had to be laid in a particularly treacherous stretch of water. The pipe-laying vessel could only work when the wave heights were less than 1.5 metres high. Weather statistics were available that gave the probability of particular wave heights for each month. An example for June is shown below:

Wave height in metres	<0.5	0.5 – 1	1 – 1.5	1.5 – 2	>2
Non-cumulative probability (%)	20	25	40	10	5
Cumulative probability (%)	20	45	85	95	100

This data can be added straight into the model as a custom distribution, usually in either non-cumulative or in cumulative form.

In non-cumulative form, the values are entered as shown in the table above. When sampling, the simulation will treat individual element in the table as a mini-uniform distribution. In our example above, 40% of our sample should lie between 1 and 1.5 metres, and will be evenly spread between these extremes.

Normal distributions

Normal distributions are bell shaped curves which tend to represent many natural events, such as the spread of results during an examination. Normal distributions are not used very frequently but are defined as a function of the mean value, and the standard deviation. One problem with using the normal distribution is that the data we wish to enter is skewed towards the pessimistic values. The normal distribution is, by definition, symmetrical. We also have to take account of the possibility that negative values may be sampled, which is usually not sensible if we are talking about costs or durations.

Summary

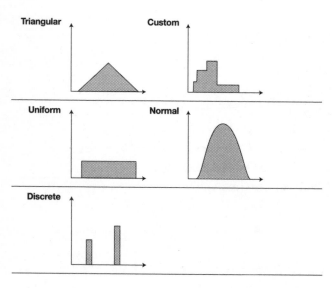

Branches

Branches are alternative routes that the model can take depending on a set of pre-defined circumstances. For example, you may be able to travel to work by car or train, and these would constitute two alternative branches. You prefer to take the train during bad weather or when you know there are going to be road works.

There are two types of branch: a probabilistic branch and a conditional branch. The branch used in the example above is a conditional branch, the 'train' branch being selected based on the condition of the weather or roads. It is more common to find conditional branches in schedule models where a particular route is dependent on the completion of a previous activity. For example, a railway construction project may involve extensive track laying and the construction of a tunnel, as shown in the site map below:

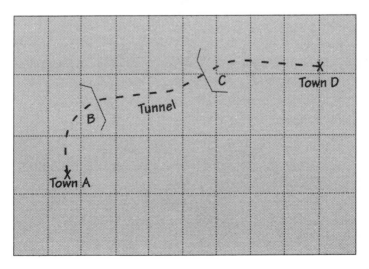

The project manager has planned to start laying the track from town A, at the same time as starting work on the tunnel B-C. If everything goes according to schedule, the tunnel will be completed by the time the tracklayers get to the beginning of the tunnel at B. However, there is a risk that the tunnel works will be delayed. In this case the tracklayers would have to move all their equipment to town D, and start working back from D to B, further delaying the project by the time that is required to get the equipment to town D.

This is shown diagrammatically in the figure below:

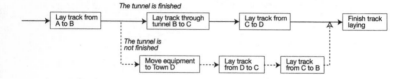

The other type of branch, a probabilistic branch, selects the route to be taken on the basis of its estimated likelihood. Probabilistic branches are used often on test activities. For example, if your project involve software development, there will be periodic tests. There is always a chance that the software will fail the test and have to be corrected and re-tested, as shown below:

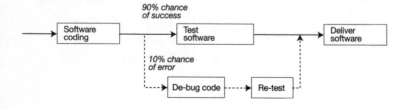

When using branches of either type, be particularly diligent in checking that they are working correctly. Both the leading software tools for undertaking schedule analysis have quite tricky rules for applying branches, and an incorrect branch can severely affect the results.

Correlation
Correlation is a method of linking distributions for items that are affected by the same set of circumstances. For example, if we have two similar activities being undertaken by the same team and we're not sure how long the tasks will take, it is a fairly safe bet that if the team discover the first task is harder than anticipated and takes longer than expected, they will also take longer to complete the second task.

In some software packages we can also apply partial correlation. This means that the results for both activities won't be exactly the same (full correlation) but will be similar.

Partial correlation tends to be more realistic since the activities are unlikely to take exactly the same time: the weather conditions may be better, or the team may have learnt the pitfalls of undertaking the task. Using partial correlation, which is usually set as a number between 0 (no correlation) and 1 (full correlation), if the first activity took five days the second activity might take anywhere from four days to six days.

Negative correlation can also usually be defined. An example of this is the correlation between the manpower resources allocation to an activity and the length of time it takes: the more resources used, the quicker it's finished.

Available software tools

There are many tools on the market that claim to model risks. However, only three really stand out as being fairly easy to use, yet powerful enough to give an accurate representation of your model. They all piggyback on other spreadsheet or project planning programmes. The selection of the simulation tool may depend to a large extent on what your organisation already uses to estimate projects.

The first I will mention is the most comprehensive and expensive, Monte Carlo from Primavera. The software works with either programme management software tools, P3 or Suretrak. It is extremely good for undertaking schedule risk assessments and can undertake a fully integrated cost and schedule analysis when used with P3.

Most users prefer a spreadsheet approach to cost assessments and @Risk for Excel based on Microsoft Excel is the best around. @Risk for MSProject, based on Microsoft Project, is also available for schedule analysis. Both versions are produced by Palisade and have to be bought individually.

@Risk for Excel is extremely easy to use, and the recent version has much improved reporting function. The distributions can be referenced to cells. @Risk for MSProject is not as easy to use, and requires long and complicated functions to be typed into a text field to represent the distributions. Both versions of @Risk are very memory intensive and, particularly with the MSProject version, it may limit the size of your model.

The last recommended product is Crystal ball, which works with Microsoft Excel. I find this slightly harder to use than

Software package	Cost analysis	Schedule analysis	Host software
Monte Carlo	✔	✔	P3 or Suretrak from Primavera
@Risk for Excel	✔	✘	Excel from Microsoft
@Risk for MSProject	✘	✔	MSProject from Microsoft
Crystal Ball	✔	✘	Excel from Microsoft

@Risk but it has some better features, such as a colour coding system for cells to indicate whether they are distributions or outputs, and more user control over the outputs. You can purchase a normal version or a professional version – for the specific differences contact your software supplier.

Model setting

The last thing we should touch upon today is the common setting of the software packages. There are three main control settings:

- Root
- Iterations
- Sample type

The Root
The simulation is based on the selection of random numbers. Computers cannot actually produce totally random numbers and use complicated algorithms in order to generate pseudo random numbers.

This is actually good news for risk analysts; it means that the results are completely repeatable, as long as the model hasn't changed and you use the same number of iterations and root. The root is the starting point for the algorithm which produces the random numbers.

Iterations

The number of iterations relates to the number of times the software will run through the simulation. Before the onset of hi tech PCs and cheap memory, it could take hours to run through five hundred iterations of a very moderately sized model; now with Pentium processors the same simulation can be performed in seconds.

The ultimate objective is to get a stable set of results. This is normally achieved by trial and error. First, run the simulation with the recommended three thousand iterations and save the summary statistics, such as the results at main percentiles, 10, 20, 30, etc. Then re-run the simulation with a changed root (see above) and compare the new results. If the new results are substantially different, then the model is not yet stable and you should increase the number of iterations.

Some software applications measure the convergence of the results and will automatically halt the simulation when the results converge within a predetermined percentage.

Sample type

Most, if not all, software packages give the user a choice between using Monte Carlo or Latin Hypercube sampling. Monte Carlo is the traditional method where random samples are selected across the entire range of the input distribution. Latin Hypercube, on the other hand, divides the distribution into a number of sections and then ensures that samples are taken from each section in turn.

Latin Hypercube will give a more uniform look to the results. It has been designed to get more stable results with less iterations. In contrast, some people would argue that it is not random enough and consequently the results are not as realistic as they might be. An example of two simulations with the same number of iterations, one using Monte Carlo and one using Latin Hypercube, is given below.

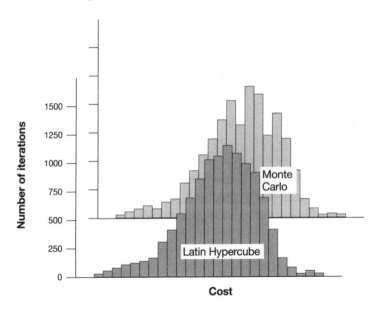

Summary

Author's recommendation: use Monte Carlo with P3 if you can afford it; or Suretrak, if you are watching your budget, for the schedule analysis; and @Risk for Excel for the cost risk analysis.

Analysing the results

Today we will look at how to:

> * Interpret the results
> * Produce several key diagrams which we can use to assist our understanding of the results.

We have now collected the information, produced our risk model and run it. So our next step is to understand what we have discovered.

I always consider that a risk assessment should tell a story, and the data presented is normally selected to support the narrative. Our plot has been developing since Monday and your role as a risk analyst is to show the project manager the 'big picture'. In order to see the big picture, you must avoid getting stuck in the detail. Keep stepping back and looking at how all the parts come together. This is quite easy to say but very difficult to do, though it will come with practice.

It is quite common for project managers to become stuck in a mental rut, with a particular pet concern or specific worry getting blown out of proportion. This can often hide many of the real issues. Test all your pet concerns with the question 'Is this a symptom or a cause?' If it's a symptom, look for the cause.

Some typical story lines that I have come across are:

- The project where all the individual team members are very competent and diligently getting on with their work. They are all very independent individuals who believe that their own area is the key to the successful delivery of the project.

  However, the risk lies in their inability to 'stitch' the parts of the project together and their failure to communicate with each other. When the individual parts do not connect efficiently the organisation rapidly deteriorates into a blame culture: 'There's nothing wrong with my bit, it's their bits that don't work properly'.

- Another common story line is where the whole project is hanging on a single 'key' assumption. There is an understanding that no one can dare challenge the assumption, as to do so will ruin the business case and effectively kill the project: 'This of course is based on the assumption that house prices continue to rise by 15% per year.'

I hope that during the course of this week you will already have a feel for where the real issues lie on your project. Unfortunately, being the harbinger of bad news is part of your job. The secret is to try and identify some of the solutions, or at least a direction in which the solution can be found.

In the rest of this chapter, I will try to give you a range of reports and charts that can be used to give you some ideas of what to look out for. As usual, we will tackle the qualitative side first. Although, I have scheduled all the report writing for Friday, a lot of the work you do today can be included in the report you will write tomorrow.

Qualitative reports

We can approach the qualitative reports from two main directions: general themes and individual critical risks.

First, we have the general themes, which could lead to a strategic level mitigation plan; a high level approach that will affect the whole project, such as a change in contracting policy; or even a re-evaluation of the project's priorities.

We can start this process by giving a general risk rating for the project. This can be done by plotting the number of risks, which fall into our high, medium and low impacts.

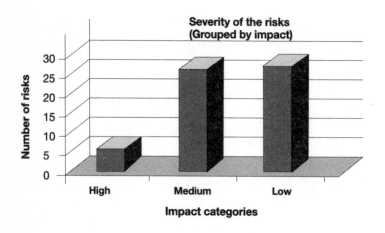

Risk categories

On Tuesday, we grouped our risks by common themes; we can now use these categories to plot the risks against meaningful comparators.

The main fields we identified were Category, Phase and WBS. By plotting the number of risks identified within each area you can build up a risk profile.

The height of the bars shows the number of risk identified and the profile shows us which phases have the greatest number of identified risks. From the chart below, we can see that the team is fairly confident in its design activities but pretty nervous when it comes to testing and roll-out. It is likely that many of the mitigation actions required to reduce the number of risks in the testing and roll out will be applied to the design and coding phases.

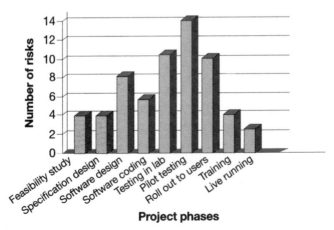

Risk Profile for a Software Development Project

However, we should ask the question: *'Is the highest bar the area with the highest risk, or just the area in which it is easiest to identify risks?'*

It is recommended that you identify between thirty and fifty risks and you may want to display the results as percentages. The chart will then show the relative number of risks in each area. When showing general risk trends, you want to lead your audience away from counting numbers and trying to spot individual risks items.

Another way of slicing and dicing the data is to consider the severity of the areas. To do this we can refer back to our Probability–Impact matrix which we developed on Tuesday.

Probability–Impact Matrix

Probability			
High	4	7	9
Medium	2	6	8
Low	1	3	5
	Low	Medium	High

Impact

Instead of using just the number of risks, we can now sum the risk scores.

Whereas in the paragraph before, it was *suggested* that you could convert the number of risks to a percentage, here it is *strongly recommended*. The scoring system is only used to help sort the risks into order of comparative severity.

Note: the total value, ie the sum of all the risks in the project, is a completely meaningless number.

One more factor has to be taken into consideration with this chart. It is possible the chart will be biased, due to the number of risks in a particular category. For example, if we had one risk in category A with a score of nine, it could look less important than category B, which has ten risks each with a score of one. When is comes to a risk management perspective, category A is far more important than B. This bias can be compensated by dividing the risk score by the number of risks in the category.

Essentially, the selection of which way to present the data is a judgement the risk analyst has to make. Keep thinking of the story and looking at each option.

The example below demonstrates this concept. The bar chart displayed in the corner (insert) shows, for each category, the percentage contribution to the total risk, taking into consideration, not the number of risks, but the score of the risks. The main chart, however, takes the weighted score of each category, hence reducing the effect of categories with large numbers of risks appearing prominent through volume rather than severity.

We can see that the charts show some quite considerable differences, which can be explained.

The insert shows that the majority of risk fall into the Political, Management and Execution categories, which reflects the concerns associated with undertaking this project in a hostile environment, such as a country in the Middle East.

The main chart, however, shows that the Scope category, although it only has three risks (ten percent of the total

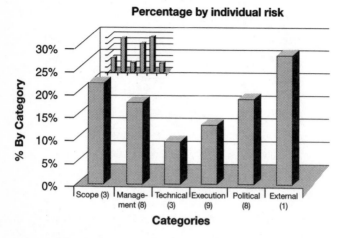

Percentage by individual risk

number identified), accounts for twenty percent of the risk. This indicates that the project is concerned that the work content may be much greater than anticipated.

You will probably produce many graphs and charts, some of which won't tell you anything. The secret is to recognise the patterns and the main themes. Just keeping asking yourself:

- What can I tell from this chart?
- Is my theory true or is it a distortion caused by the way I plotted the data?
- Can I test my theory by any other means?

Control

One of the other fields we collected was the Controllability. This indicates the level of influence that the project has over the risk. In its simplest form, we can look at the risk score for each of the three categories, Control, Influence and None.

We can become more sophisticated by combining the controllability chart with the Source versus Bearer chart. In our data collection phase, we recorded who was the source of the risk and who suffered the consequences.

		Client	Project team	Suppliers	Manufacturers	External	
Source	Client	5	10		1		Each box displays the number of risks
	Project team	1	34	4			
	Suppliers	5	12				
	Manufacturers	2	10				
	External		5				

Bearer (column header group)

This can be combined with controllability to determine which of the risks in the matrix we have most influence over.

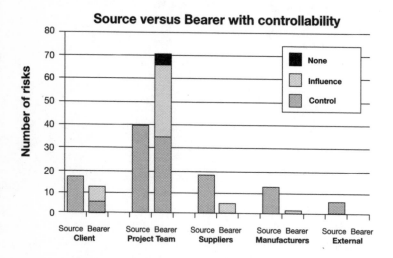

Source versus Bearer with controllability

I have to admit that there aren't many projects in which this chart is particularly useful. However, there is a current trend for organisations to engage sub-contractors in partnership agreements. This is generally done when the scope is clear but the cost or effort is not. By agreeing a target price with a risk and reward mechanism for coming within budget or overspending, the client can be assured that the contractor is motivated to cut costs rather than run up a large bill. In such cases, it is vital to know exactly where each risk lies and such a diagram can form part of the contract, where responsibilities for managing risks are clearly assigned.

Critical risks

Up to now we have been looking at the general health of the

project, and trying to identify common themes running through the identified risks. We should also focus on the most serious risks. The way we can determine these top risks is to refer back to the P-I Matrix and select bands.

Probability–Impact Matrix

		Low	Medium	High
Probability	High	4	7	9
	Medium	2	6	8
	Low	1	3	5
		Low	Medium	High

Impact

A system that worked well for me on previous projects was to deem all risks scoring eight or more as critical risks, requiring immediate action. Those scoring five or more I termed significant risks, requiring the preparation of mitigation plans. The rest were to be monitored only.

Quantitative results

The quantitative results can be broken into two areas, and it will depend on the culture of your organisation as to where the emphasis lies.

Cost

There are three important facts we want to establish:

1 What is our chance of achieving the target or budget?

2 How much contingency do we need?
3 How do the major risks affect the cost?

Chance of achieving the budget
I am afraid that the answer to our first question is probably going to be quite negative; it is the nature of a risk analysis to look for risks rather than opportunities. It is easy to forget that there is a whole project team working to prevent these risks from occurring.

Once you have determined that there is little chance of meeting your budget, you should break down the costs to get a better view of where you are likely to overrun. The concept of cost centres is quite useful and can be displayed on a table, as shown below for an oil and gas project.

Cost centres	Target	% Chance	P20	Expected	P80
Design	300	30%	220	450	650
Rig platform	12,000	27%	10,678	13,789	14,500
Rig topsides	4,500	<1%	4,550	5,200	6,400
Hook up and commissioning	340	94%	270	300	330
Drilling programme	1,200	25%	1,100	1,425	1,500

The table above looks at the main components of the construction of an oil rig. Even although only one of the elements seems to have a good chance of meeting the budget, the main worry should lie with the topsides.

The topsides are the processing and drilling equipment that sit on the rig's platform, and in our case it seems that the target estimate is extremely low. This should be revisited to get a more realistic figure, as the analysis predicts a less than 1% chance of the target budget being achieved.

Contingency levels

The contingency level can be set by using the 'S'-Curve. The organisation normally takes a corporate view on how much money should be put aside to cover the possibility of things going wrong. I hope that the risk analysis has now identified most of the things that could go wrong and factored them into the model.

If we look again at the 'S'–Curve, I have marked three lines: the target cost, (which has around a thirty percent chance of being achieved), the P50 (fifty percent) and the P80 (eighty percent).

A widely used system, is to identify two contingency levels: a local level which is held by the project manager, and a company level which is held by the board of directors.

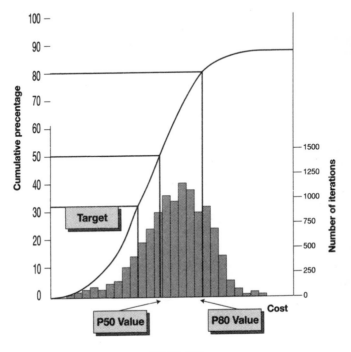

It is still the objective of the project manager to meet or better the target. However, the board, being realistic, knows that the project is likely to cost more. Usually they pick something around the P50 mark. Anything below this value is a bonus and the project manager should be rewarded appropriately.

The board of directors also has to consider the possibility of the project going badly awry and have to set aside funds for this eventuality. Because it is unlikely that every single risk will occur and that the project manager would do nothing to mitigate the risks as they impacted, the P80 is often selected.

Major risk impacts
The third point probably requires scenario testing, a sort of 'What if?' analysis.

It is often a good idea to take the top risks and rerun the model, first setting them to a 100% likelihood and then setting them to a 0% likelihood. This will show you how the overall cost could be affected by the occurrence of each of these risks. It can also be a guide as to how much money you should invest in mitigation.

If the expected difference in cost between, including and excluding the risk is substantial, then you can afford to invest a percentage of the difference on ensuring that the risk has a much lower likelihood of occurrence.

Schedule

On many large projects, the cost impacts are driven by the schedule. For example in oil and gas projects the time it takes to get what is termed 'First Oil' is critical, or in the pharmaceutical business, the critical factor is to get the product to market.

There are four main questions we want to answer:

1 What is the chance of achieving the target end date?
2 What is the chance of achieving our critical milestones?
3 What are the main critical paths?
4 How much float do I have, if any?

The first question is our main lead; if by chance the project is going to achieve the end date easily, we can relax. However, it is much more likely that the schedule targets are aggressive and have a less than 50% chance of being achieved.

The easiest way to view these results is by using a Time Summary Chart, very similar to our Cost Summary Chart, only this time looking at either specific dates or durations. The chart below shows a typical project with a very low chance of achieving its target.

It is possible that you have not quite agreed on a start date, so

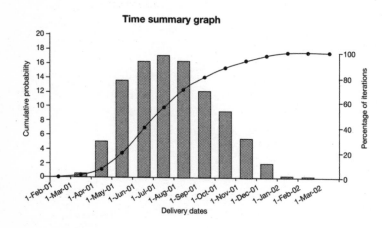

Time summary graph

the same information can be displayed with durations rather than actual dates.

OK, now we know we have a problem. We can now stop panicking and try to find out why. The next two items should help us to do this.

Milestones

All good projects should be broken down into milestones, preferably not less than ten or no more than 15.

We can then undertake the above analysis on each of the major milestones, looking at the chance of achieving each one in turn. This should identify where the project goes adrift.

The chart below shows the 'key' milestones of a shipbuilding project. The milestones are shown on the left hand side and the bars stretch from the earliest date a milestone could finish to the latest date. The joint in the middle of each bar shows the expected date of the milestone.

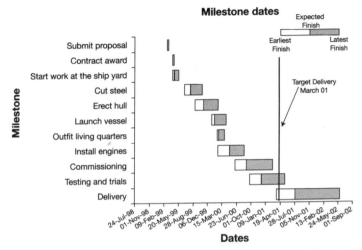

The chart shows that there is a very slim chance of delivering on time; it is likely to be about four months late. It appears that the problems lie with the commissioning phase, since that milestone has a significantly longer bar than the other milestones. Based on this chart, the project should concentrate on minimising the risks to the commissioning activities.

Critical paths
The critical path is the longest route through the project from start to finish. Let us take as an example the activities required to build a house:

- Identify a site
- Buy the site
- Hire an architect
- Produce the basic plans
- Apply for planning permission
- Hire a builder
- Build the house.

Bearing in mind that this is a much simplified list, I can list the activities in the order I want to do them, in a project plan as shown below:

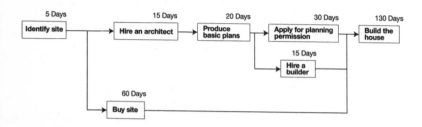

I have decided to do quite a lot of work before I have completed the purchase of the site; this could definitely be considered a high-risk strategy on cost, but it will save me time.

I can estimate durations for each of the activities, and it appears that I have three main routes through my network, prior to the start of the building work.

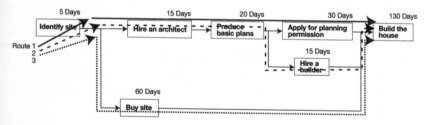

Route 1 will take 70 days, route 2 will take 55 days, and route 3 will take 65 days.

From our quick calculation of durations, route 1 is our critical path. Using traditional project management, the project manager would concentrate on the activities that ran along route 1. However, using risk analysis, we could apply risks to all of the activities, such as 'Difficulties in determining ownership of the land' or 'The economic climate leads to a shortage in qualified builders'. Either of these risks could change the critical path.

Most risk assessment packages will print out a list of the individual activity's criticality. This is expressed as a percentage, representing the number of times that a particular activity would appear on the critical path during a hundred iterations.

Activity	Criticality
Identify site	100
Hire an architect	60
Produce basic plans	60
Apply for planning permission	45
Hire a builder	15
Buy site	40
Start work	100

This shows the project manager that he or she cannot afford to ignore the activities that do not lie on the obvious critical path. However, the selection of builder is not as critical as the site purchase or the application for planning permission.

This information can also be shown graphically, particularly when you have several clear routes. The example below has been taken from an oil and gas project. It was used to demonstrate to the customer that he was the most critical dependency.

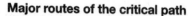
Major routes of the critical path

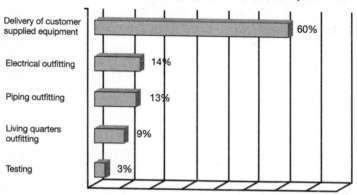

Scenario testing

Again, on the schedule side as well as the cost side, we can look at scenario testing to see if we can undertake different options that would increase our chances of completing the project on time. We could decide to reduce the scope or functionality, or just change the order in which we do things.

A classic example of this is in the outfitting of ships. Outfitting is the process of putting all the insides onto a ship, such as the furniture, wiring or plumbing. Quite often, if a project is running behind, they decide to carry out the outfitting at sea whilst delivering the vessel. The standard ratio of outfitting at sea as opposed to outfitting at the dock is three to one. So if you had a vessel being built in the UK but being delivered to, say Singapore, it may take six weeks to deliver it. If the outfitting was planned to take two weeks at the dock side, the project manager could well argue that the outfitting could be done at sea and would be complete by the time the vessel arrived at its destination. It doesn't often work, but it is often tried.

A chart of a scenario comparison can be seen below.

Time summary graph – comparing scenario with base case

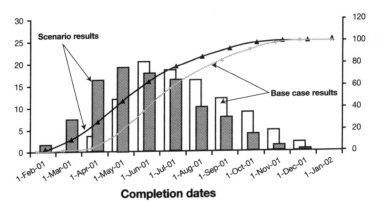

Completion dates

The darker bars show the results of the scenario and the lighter bars show the result of the base case. We can see that the scenario could save the project about two months which, depending on the cost, would probably be worth doing.

Combined

The cost and schedule analysis can be combined to ensure that we consider the project in its entirety and we do not sacrifice cost for schedule or vice versa. There are two ways of doing this – the first is to look at a sensitivity analysis.

Some of the advanced software packages can do this automatically; the package compares the results with the inputs and tries to infer which inputs have the greatest effect on the results. For example, if nearly every time there is a cost overrun there is an overrun of the schedule.

At this point, you should also perform what is colloquially known as a 'sanity check' and re-evaluate the register scores against the quantitative results. For example, the top risk in the register may be 'Political intervention'. We can now see, from the sensitivity analysis above, that it has little effect on the overall outcome of the project. Therefore, you might downgrade the risk in light of the quantitative results.

Advanced analysis

Some risk assessments are conducted as evaluation tools to determine whether a project is worth pursuing. In such cases, reporting measures such as the net present value of the project or the internal rate of return can be used. Most packages can produce such outputs as long as there is an integrated cost and schedule model.

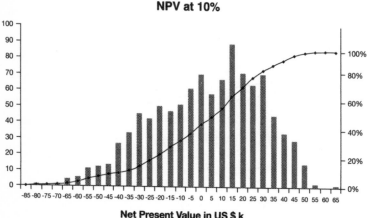

NPV at 10%

Net Present Value in US $ k

The graph above shows the results of such a project for a company that insists on a minimum return of fourteen percent. It looks unlikely that this project will go ahead as it is right on the balance point, which could indicate some manipulation of the spreadsheet to give a positive result. Such an analysis tends to highlight proposals that have been tailored to meet the organisation's hurdle rates.

Summary

You should now have all the key components of a risk assessment – both qualitative and quantitative. We know how much the project is likely to cost, when we expect it to finish, what could go wrong, and why.

You should now have a useful guide on what should be done about it. Now you have to sell your conclusions to the boss.

Producing a report

From the work we carried out yesterday, we know the main story of this project. We must now tell this story to the sponsor of the assessment who might be the project manager, the board of directors or a senior manager.

Even if you, as the project manager, sponsored the assessment to give yourself peace of mind, it is a good idea to write up the results. Each analysis refers to a snapshot in time and it is probable that another assessment will be carried out in a few months. This report will form the basis of any future analysis, by comparing future analyses you can tell whether the situation is improving or worsening.

The report you produce must deliver a clear message: 'This project is in good health with a few minor remedial actions required', or 'This project is in crisis with urgent action required'.

The report should also include what you did, how you mapped the risks, and to whom you talked. In this way the reader can make informed judgements about the quality of the results. A suggested format is shown below; the report being divided into six sections.

Introduction
The introduction should include a short description of the project and the reason for undertaking the risk assessment.

Method
The method is really the details of the steps that you have taken previously this week. It tells the reader how you gathered the data, assessed the impact of the risks, mapped the risks onto the risk model and evaluated the results.

Once you have conducted your first risk assessment on a project, you can use the same section as a basis for your subsequent reports, or you can simply refer directly to the first report.

Source of information
This section lists the data sources, and would typically include a list of the brainstorming attendees, who was interviewed and when, a reference to the cost estimate you used, and the plan on which you based the schedule risk model.

This section can also include a list of assumptions that you made in undertaking the analysis. This ensures that your reader is clearly aware of what is and isn't included in the analysis.

Assumptions can be useful in taking out some of the variability from the results, thus making it easier to interpret the results of the analysis. If an assumption is challenged, it can always form the basis of a 'what if' sensitivity analysis, where the impact of the assumption itself can be assessed.

For example, if we have assumed that a key component will be delivered on time, we can run a couple of 'what if' scenarios showing the component being 1, 2 or several weeks late.

Results
This is where you provide the findings of the analysis, and it is good idea to divide the findings into qualitative and quantitative.

In the qualitative section you should provide as a *minimum*:

- A risk matrix
- A list of the 'top ten' risks

But don't forget all those charts we produced yesterday.

For the quantitative analysis, the *minimum* should include:

- Cost summary chart(s)
- Time summary chart(s)
- A list (or bar chart) showing which activities are critical.

But don't forget breaking down the costs by cost centres, analysis of intermediate milestones and the sensitivity analyses. You could also include some 'what-if' scenarios, to demonstrate that you have thought about the main issues.

Conclusion
The conclusion section is your opportunity to spell out the findings from the results section, with hopefully some rationale for your statements.

Some common conclusions are along the lines of:

- This project only has an x % chance of being completed on or before the target date.
- It is likely that the estimate will be exceeded before the revenue is realised.
- There is a high risk that component 'Y' will not be delivered on time.

Recommendations

Whereas the conclusions generally contain the bad news, the recommendations should contain the good news. They should tell us what can be done to minimise the impacts that are likely to occur. In the worst case, this will relate to re-planning or estimating to accept the change in circumstances. Quite often the conclusions and recommendation sections are merged, particularly if you want to relate particular recommendations with individual conclusions.

Depending on the length of the report, it may be a good idea to include a summary after the introduction section. This would include the main results, such as the cost results and the expected duration of the project, with a list of the main conclusions and recommendations.

Summary

You now have a comprehensive document which you can present to your sponsors. It would also be a good idea to produce a 25 minute presentation of the results, as you will almost certainly be asked to give one to explain your findings.

What next?

With the week coming to a close, we wrap things up by looking at how to:

> - Undertake immediate action to reduce the impact of the critical risks
> - Produce a risk management plan, to outline a process for the ongoing management of risk during the life of the project.

So assuming a few problems do exist, the board or project manager will want to know what to do next. Two main steps can now be taken to set the project back on the right track.

The first is to identify those risk items that are critical, that is require urgent action to prevent disaster; and the second is to set in place a process for the ongoing management of risk. The risk management plan is simply a document that instructs the team members as to how they will formally manage risk within their project.

Action plans for critical risk items

You will remember from Thursday that we plotted our risks
on a P-I matrix, and we also defined the controllability of
each of those risks. We stated that those risks that scored nine
were deemed critical, ie require immediate action, and those
that scored over six were significant and should have action
plans in place.

Probability–Impact Matrix

We should now concentrate, at least, on the critical risks and
develop an action plan to reduce or mitigate each of them. We
also discussed on Tuesday the four types of mitigation plans
we could consider: transfer, eliminate, mitigate and accept.

The key difference now between the mitigation plan and the
action plan is that the mitigation plan is something that could
be undertaken to reduce the risks on an ongoing basis,
whereas the action plan is something that we must do *now* to
reduce the risk.

The type of mitigation that we can apply will depend on the
amount of influence the project has over the risk; this is
shown in the table below:

Mitigating actions

Controllability		Transfer	Eliminate	Mitigate	Accept
	Control		✔	✔	✔
	Influence	✔		✔	✔
	None	✔			✔

What we want to do is set down a series of tasks that an individual within the organisation is responsible for carrying out. The affect of the tasks can be included in the model and the model re-run. If the risk is significantly reduced then the plan is worth implementing. This decision can help assess the benefit of the actions. If the mitigation plan is carried out, we should revisit the assessment to ensure that the risk severity or probability has been reduced. Say, for example, we have a risk that the access to the construction site may be unsuitable for large equipment. In order to mitigate the risk, we can ask a member of the project team to carry out a detailed survey of the access road. If the road is unsuitable, he should consider other possible solutions such as alternative modes of access, eg sea or air, or construction of a more suitable road to the site.

It is very easy to think that writing a mitigating action is the same as the action being undertaken and many projects fall victim to risks which were identified well in advance, but no action was taken.

The action plan should include:

- Identifying who is responsible for completing the action
- When it should be completed
- The trigger points when the individual is required to report back to the project manager for further decisions

- How much money should be committed to undertake the action
- Forecast the reduction of risk against the cost of the action.

Forms can be produced for each of the critical risks, like the one shown below:

Risk 43: Access Road for heavy equipment	Score 9: Critical
Description: The access road to the site may not support heavy equipment such as cranes and lorries required to undertake the building works.	**Actionee:** _____ **To be completed by:** _____ **Budget:** _____
Mitigation action: Undertake a survey of the access road, assume standard 40 tonne articulated trucks and crane suitable for a 100 ft 75 tonne vertical lift.	**Approved by:** _____ _____
Predicted score after mitigation: 1	**ON COMPLETION** **Date completed:** _____
Secondary risk: Access road determined unsuitable.	**Cost:** _____
Secondary mitigation action: • Investigate alternative access, ie sea and air. • Upgrade existing access road.	**Risk score:** _____ **Secondary risks:** _____

How to create a risk management plan

Depending on the size of the project, you will have to decide on the level of risk management that you wish to implement. Whatever your decision, you should produce a risk management plan to communicate the level of risk management to the rest of the project and to the project sponsors.

One extreme may be to undertake no formal risk management, leaving the role to the everyday intuitions of the project manager and task leaders. The other extreme would be a dedicated team, who would have no other function in the project.

Resourcing issues
The level of resourcing for risk management depends on the overall budget of the project and the degree of risk. From my experience, an average project with a budget of under £100,000 does not require a full-time risk manager. However, the project team should be briefed on risk management and a very simple risk recording mechanism should be set up to ensure that all the risks have been considered.

Projects from £100,000 to £1 million should consider combining the risk management role with an existing role – the QA function and planning function are common candidates. However, if the project manager has an assistant then this usually proves to be a very good solution.

Projects from £1 million to £50 million frequently have a member of the project with responsibility for risk management, supported by periodic risk assessments, normally carried out by independent consultants.

Projects over £50 million should have a dedicated resource specifically undertaking risk management. This resource should report directly to the project manager.

Projects over £250 million are normally defined as programmes, a series of smaller projects with a common aim. In programmes, it is normal to have a risk team as part of the programme office or programme controls function.

Producing the plan

Once you have identified your structure, you can determine what you want the people to do. This will be very dependent on the level of resources. This can be an iterative process; if you identify too much work for a part time role, or you can see synergies with other roles in the team, you can adjust your resource requirements accordingly.

Some organisations will have templates for producing plans. Someone else has already considered the contents so as to form a uniform corporate standard; all you have to do is add the detail.

Suggested contents

The plans should be clear and simple to follow. You should also consider not just the process of managing risk, but the process of ensuring that the risks are being managed – the dreaded audit function.

A good starting point would be as follows:

Risk Management Plan

- Introduction
- Scope
- Definitions
- Responsibilities
- Procedures
- Related Documents

A risk management plan can be anything from six to 60 pages. But remember, project managers are busy people and it will be hard enough to get them to read six pages let alone 60.

Suggested contents for each section

Here are some ideas for the contents of each section.

Introduction
The introduction should explain to the reader why the project feels the need to manage risk using a formal process. This will be followed by a quick overview as to the design process, i.e. whose idea was the document, who wrote it, and when was it written. And don't forget to mention the objectives of the Risk Assessment.

Scope
The scope defines the boundary of the plan; it makes it clear to the reader the limits of authority. The scope is normally something like:

> All known risks having a potential impact on the project's objectives will be assessed. Risks are to be considered in terms of their impact to the project, whether or not the liability for the risk lies with project team.

The risk 'ownership' section of the risk register will identify the organisation individual, department or functional group responsible.

So this implies that the plan will not address business or organisational risks that do not affect the project's objectives. In these days of share price sensitivity and ecological pressure groups, this narrow view may not be acceptable to the organisation.

Definitions
This section describes exactly what is meant by the

terminology used within the documents. We have already come across our definition of risk on Monday.

You can also briefly define what is meant by any other terms used in the document, such as the project, the organisation, the client, etc.

Responsibilities

This is an indication of who is supposed to do what. Again, a nice clear description is needed so that the risk manager, or project manager, can pick up the plan and understand what it is he or she is expected to be contributing. The type roles that should be defined here are:

- Project manager
- Risk manager
- Team member
- Risk nominee
- Risk action owner
- Client

An example for the risk nominee would be:

The risk nominee

The risk nominee is responsible for the management of a particular risk. The risk nominee is the individual most able to manage the risk and to best understand its importance and implications.
The risk nominee is responsible for identifying the risk management actions and selecting the action owners. Risk nominees should be members of the project team where possible, but may be appointed from organisations outside the project team.

In summary, the risk nominee shall:
* be assigned for each identified risk by the project manager;
* actively co-ordinate the risk management actions for his or her assigned risks;
* monitor the implementation and report on the progress of the mitigating actions.

By using a definitions section you can clearly lay out what exactly you mean by the different roles. Whether the term 'risk manager' is a good or bad one doesn't really matter, as long as it is clearly defined in the plan.

Procedures
This section is like the equivalent of this book, describing the detailed steps that have to be undertaken to conduct the ongoing process of risk management.

Quite often it is a good idea to draw out the process in a diagram and to reference each box in the diagram to a section of the plan, like the process chart shown on the next page.

The only box that we have not touched on during this week's gallop through risk assessment is the management box.

Here you should consider the day-to-day role of the risk manager;

* arranging review meetings
* reporting on progress of the risk mitigation actions
* sending out action reminders
* getting the risk owners to update the register.

Whether you have a fulltime risk manager or not, someone in the team should be given the responsibility for undertaking these actions.

Appendices
Appendices may contain a set of forms that can be filled in by project members to raise risks, or references to other plans within the project documentation, such as the quality, issue or assumptions plan.

The risk management plan could also detail the tools that you intend to use during the process. These will include the software packages you intend to use. Perhaps you will also

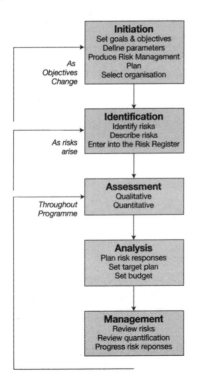

want to mandate the standards for the production of risk friendly budgets and schedules.

Summary

Now you should be in the position of having allocated the critical risks to the project team and written the risk management plan. All you have to do now is get into the routine of:

- Identifying risks
- Assessing their impact
- Assigning actions
- Reviewing progress
- Reporting to the project manager.

Your project manager can now relax in the sure knowledge that everything is being taken care of, and all the risks to his or her objectives have been covered.